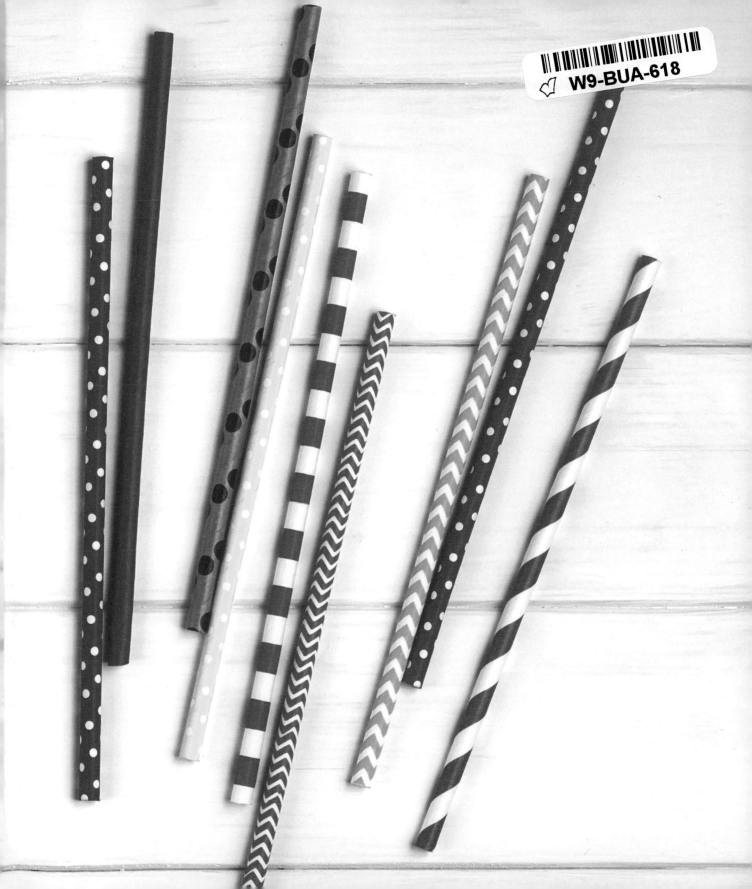

JUICE
BAR

healthy juices
& smoothies

pil

Publications International, Ltd.

CONTENTS

JUICE BAR BASICS

Turn your kitchen into your favorite juice bar with easy recipes for delicious juices and smoothies. These drinks are fast, flavorful and fun—but that's not why they're so popular. They make you feel good! Fruits and vegetables provide so many nutritional benefits that you just can't get from a bowl of cereal—or even a vitamin supplement. From hydrating your body and boosting energy levels to improving digestion and helping prevent diseases, juices and smoothies can provide an impressive array of health benefits. They're a convenient way to fit more fruits and vegetables into your daily diet—and you'll be getting all the nutrients in their natural form, with no added ingredients or labels to read.

GETTING STARTED

Whether you choose a juicer or a blender, you'll want to use organic produce whenever possible. Wash all produce before juicing or blending, and remove any bruised or blemished parts. Some fruits and vegetables, such as oranges, grapefruit, kiwis, pineapples, jicamas and sweet potatoes, should be peeled before using.

DRINK THE RAINBOW

Use as many different colors of produce as possible to ensure that you're getting a wide variety of nutrients. (They don't all have to go in the juicer or blender at the same time!) Balance your fruit and vegetable intake—if you're drinking juices or smoothies daily, try starting with at least two-thirds vegetables in your drinks to keep the sugar content under control. Add fruits for sweetness, along with spices and/or a small amount of natural sweeteners such as honey or maple syrup.

ALL THE EXTRAS

Boost the flavor and nutritional value of your juices and smoothies with a variety of healthful additions, including spices, seeds, powders and more.

acai berries: Most commonly found frozen, this Brazilian superfood is packed with antioxidants and fiber; it may help reduce cholesterol and blood pressure.

apple cider vinegar: With valuable probiotic and anti-inflammatory properties, this vinegar can aid in digestion and help the body maintain a healthy alkaline level. (Choose raw apple cider vinegar rather than the more widely available pasteurized version.)

bee pollen: Contains all the essential amino acids (making it a complete protein) along with vitamins and minerals.

chia seeds: Packed with fiber, protein and omega-3 fatty acids, these seeds can dramatically increase the nutritional profile of your beverages while adding a slightly nutty flavor.

coconut milk: Provides a big protein boost to smoothies while adding a mildly sweet, nutty coconut flavor. Pairs well with tropical fruits such as pineapple and mango.

coconut oil: This superfood is anti-viral, anti-fungal, full of antioxidants and can help balance blood sugar and boost metabolism.

flaxseed or flaxseed oil: A good source of protein, fiber, omega-3 fatty acids and vitamin E, flaxseed can help lower cholesterol and reduce the risk of heart disease. Purchase ground flaxseed (rather than whole) for use in beverages.

green tea powder (matcha): High in antioxidants, vitamins, minerals and amino acids, matcha may help boost metabolism and lower blood sugar.

ground red pepper or jalapeños: An anti-inflammatory containing capsaicin, this spicy addition to your drinks may boost your immune system and fire up your metabolism.

hemp seeds: An easily digestible complete protein that's also rich in Omega-3 fatty acids, iron and magnesium, hemp seeds can be blended into any smoothie or juice without altering the flavor. (Look for shelled seeds called "hemp hearts" or hemp protein powder.)

nut and seed butters: Add almond butter, peanut butter, sunflower seed butter or tahini to your smoothies for a delicious protein boost. The healthy fats and fiber in these butters help keep you feeling fuller for longer.

spirulina: Made from an aquatic plant and packed with nutrients including vitamins, minerals, omega-3 fatty acids and protein, spirulina promotes dental health and may help lower bad cholesterol while increasing good cholesterol. It's best added to green smoothies along with some sweet fruit, as many find the flavor to be somewhat unpleasant.

tofu: Blends beautifully into smoothies, adding high-quality complete protein and a creamy texture. It also pairs well with almost any ingredient.

turmeric: Promotes healthy metabolism and is also known for anti-inflammatory properties. This root vegetable can be grated into your drinks (or add ground turmeric instead); the flavor goes well with green smoothies and juice blends containing pineapple or carrots.

yogurt (preferably Greek or Icelandic): Adds a significant amount of protein and a creamy texture to your smoothies.

WAKE UP AND JUICE

TANGERAPPLE

makes 2 servings

2 apples

2 tangerines, peeled

¼ lemon, peeled

Juice apples, tangerines and lemon. Stir.

UP AND AT 'EM

makes 1 serving

2 cups loosely
  packed spinach

1 apple

1 carrot

1 stalk celery

¼ lemon, peeled

1 inch fresh ginger,
  peeled

Juice spinach, apple, carrot, celery, lemon and ginger. Stir.

SUPER C

makes 3 servings

2 oranges, peeled

1 grapefruit, peeled

1 lemon, peeled

½ cup fresh cranberries

2 teaspoons honey

Juice oranges, grapefruit, lemon and cranberries. Stir in honey until well blended.

KIWI TWIST

makes 2 servings

2 kiwis, peeled
2 pears
½ lemon, peeled

Juice kiwis, pears and lemon. Stir.

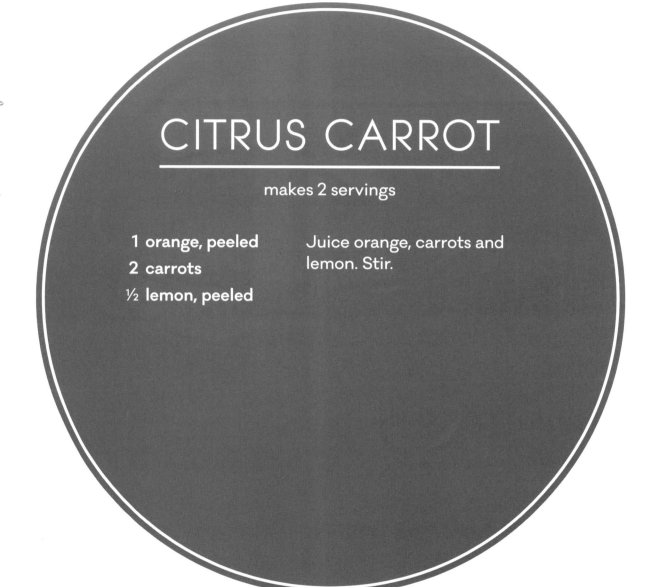

CITRUS CARROT

makes 2 servings

1 orange, peeled
2 carrots
½ lemon, peeled

Juice orange, carrots and lemon. Stir.

GREEN BOOST

makes 2 servings

1 green apple
2 stalks celery
3 leaves kale
½ cucumber
½ lemon, peeled
1 inch fresh ginger,
  peeled

Juice apple, celery, kale, cucumber, lemon and ginger. Stir.

SWEET AND SPICY CITRUS

makes 2 servings

5 carrots

1 orange or
  2 clementines,
  peeled

⅓ cup strawberries,
  hulled

1 lemon, peeled

½ inch fresh ginger,
  peeled

Juice carrots, orange,
strawberries, lemon and
ginger. Stir.

WHEATGRASS BLAST

makes 2 servings

2 apples
2 cups wheatgrass
1 lemon, peeled
6 sprigs fresh mint

Juice apples, wheatgrass, lemon and mint. Stir.

MELON RASPBERRY MEDLEY

makes 2 servings

⅛ **honeydew melon, rind removed**

⅛ **seedless watermelon, rind removed**

⅓ **cup raspberries**

Ice cubes

Juice honeydew, watermelon and raspberries. Stir. Serve over ice.

WORKOUT WARMUP

makes 2 servings

2 **apples**
2 **kiwis, peeled**
4 **leaves kale**
½ **lime, peeled**

Juice apples, kiwis, kale and lime. Stir.

START ME UP

makes 2 servings

1 orange, peeled

1 apple

½ cup raspberries

½ cup strawberries, hulled

Juice orange, apple, raspberries and strawberries. Stir.

INVIGORATING GREENS AND CITRUS

makes 2 servings

2 oranges, peeled

1 grapefruit, peeled

1 zucchini

½ cup broccoli florets

½ inch fresh ginger, peeled

Juice oranges, grapefruit, zucchini, broccoli and ginger. Stir.

MORNING BLEND

makes 2 servings

¼ pineapple, peeled

1 orange, peeled

1 inch fresh ginger, peeled

Juice pineapple, orange and ginger. Stir.

SUNRISE BERRY

makes 2 servings

1 cup strawberries, hulled

1 orange, peeled

½ lime, peeled

Juice strawberries, orange and lime. Stir.

ANTIOXIDANT BLENDS

IMMUNITY BOOSTER

makes 3 servings

1 grapefruit,
   peeled

2 oranges, peeled

½ cup blackberries

Juice grapefruit, oranges and blackberries. Stir.

GREEN REJUVENATION

makes 2 servings

2 cups loosely
packed spinach

¼ pineapple,
peeled

1 pear

1 cup fresh parsley

½ grapefruit,
peeled

Juice spinach, pineapple, pear, parsley and grapefruit. Stir.

RED CABBAGE AND PINEAPPLE

makes 2 servings

¼ **red cabbage**

¼ **pineapple, peeled**

Juice cabbage and pineapple. Stir.

COLD AND FLU NINJA JUICE

makes 1 serving

1 orange, peeled
½ lemon, peeled
⅛ small red onion
1 clove garlic
½ teaspoon honey

Juice orange, lemon, onion and garlic. Stir in honey until well blended.

CRANBERRY PEAR FUSION

makes 2 servings

2 pears

½ cucumber

¾ cup fresh or thawed frozen cranberries

¼ lemon, peeled

½ to 1 inch fresh ginger, peeled

Juice pears, cucumber, cranberries, lemon and ginger. Stir.

VITAMIN BLAST

makes 2 servings

¼ **cantaloupe, rind removed**

1 **orange, peeled**

¼ **papaya**

2 **leaves Swiss chard**

Juice cantaloupe, orange, papaya and chard. Stir.

POMEGRANATE-LIME-COCONUT JUICE

makes 2 servings

1 pomegranate, peeled

½ cucumber

1 lime, peeled

¼ cup coconut water

Juice pomegranate seeds, cucumber and lime. Stir in coconut water until well blended.

SUPER BETA-CAROTENE

makes 2 servings

4 carrots
1 apple
4 leaves bok choy
2 leaves kale
½ inch fresh ginger, peeled

Juice carrots, apple, bok choy, kale and ginger. Stir.

PEAR RASPBERRY

makes 2 servings

2 **pears**
2 **cups raspberries**
½ **cucumber**

Juice pears, raspberries and cucumber. Stir.

SUPER BERRY REFRESHER

makes 2 servings

1 cup strawberries,
   hulled

1 cup raspberries

1 cucumber

½ cup blackberries

½ cup blueberries

¼ lemon, peeled

Juice strawberries, raspberries, cucumber, blackberries, blueberries and lemon. Stir.

CLEANSING GREEN JUICE

makes 2 servings

4 leaves bok choy
1 stalk celery
½ cucumber
¼ bulb fennel
½ lemon, peeled

Juice bok choy, celery, cucumber, fennel and lemon. Stir.

CHERRY AND MELON

makes 3 servings

⅛ small watermelon, rind removed

¼ cantaloupe, rind removed

¾ cup cherries, pitted

Juice watermelon, cantaloupe and cherries. Stir.

COOL APPLE MANGO

makes 2 servings

1 mango, peeled

1 apple

1 cucumber

½ inch fresh ginger, peeled

Juice mango, apple, cucumber and ginger. Stir.

TANGY TWIST

makes 3 servings

1 grapefruit,
   peeled

4 carrots

1 apple

1 beet

1 inch fresh
   ginger, peeled

Ice cubes

Juice grapefruit, carrots, apple, beet and ginger. Stir. Serve over ice.

DRINK YOUR VEGETABLES

DOUBLE GREEN PINEAPPLE

makes 1 serving

4 leaves Swiss chard

4 leaves kale

¼ pineapple, peeled

Juice chard, kale and pineapple. Stir.

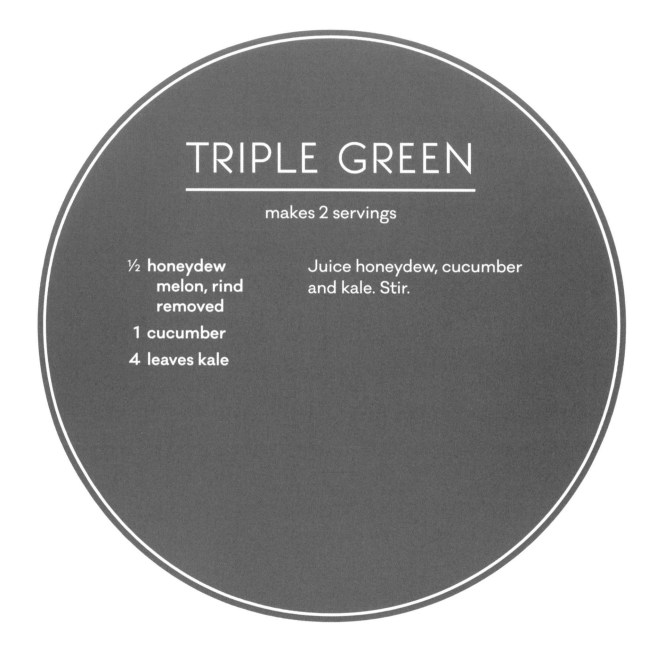

TRIPLE GREEN

makes 2 servings

½ **honeydew melon, rind removed**

1 **cucumber**

4 **leaves kale**

Juice honeydew, cucumber and kale. Stir.

PINEAPPLE-MANGO FUSION

makes 3 servings

¼ pineapple, peeled

1 mango, peeled

1 cucumber

½ lemon, peeled

Juice pineapple, mango, cucumber and lemon. Stir.

APPLE-K JUICE

makes 2 servings

1 apple
1 kiwi, peeled
4 leaves kale
1 stalk celery
½ lemon, peeled

Juice apple, kiwi, kale, celery and lemon. Stir.

CABBAGE PATCH JUICE

makes 3 servings

2 apples
¼ napa cabbage
¼ red cabbage

Juice apples, napa cabbage and red cabbage. Stir.

MINT JULEP JUICE

makes 1 serving

1 apple

1 cup loosely
   packed spinach

1 stalk celery

1 cup fresh mint

Juice apple, spinach, celery and mint. Stir.

APPLE CARROT ZINGER

makes 2 servings

4 carrots

2 apples

¼ cucumber

1 inch fresh ginger,
  peeled

Juice carrots, apples, cucumber and ginger. Stir.

GREEN ENERGY

makes 4 servings

2 apples
2 stalks celery
6 leaves kale
½ cup loosely
  packed spinach
½ cucumber
¼ bulb fennel
½ lemon, peeled
1 inch fresh ginger,
  peeled

Juice apples, celery, kale, spinach, cucumber, fennel, lemon and ginger. Stir.

WALDORF JUICE

makes 2 servings

2 apples

6 leaves beet greens, Swiss chard or kale

2 stalks celery

Juice apples, beet greens and celery. Stir.

ORANGE FENNEL SPROUT

makes 2 servings

2 oranges, peeled
2 stalks celery
1 bulb fennel
1 cup alfalfa
   sprouts

Juice oranges, celery, fennel and alfalfa sprouts. Stir.

APPLE MELON JUICE

makes 3 servings

¼ **honeydew melon, rind removed**

¼ **cantaloupe, rind removed**

1 **apple**

3 **leaves kale**

3 **leaves Swiss chard**

Juice honeydew, cantaloupe, apple, kale and chard. Stir.

SWEET
AND GREEN

makes 2 servings

1 cup broccoli
   florets

¼ pineapple,
   peeled

2 stalks celery

Juice broccoli, pineapple
and celery. Stir.

AUTUMN APPLE PIE

makes 2 servings

2 apples

½ butternut squash, peeled

¼ teaspoon pumpkin pie spice

Juice apples and squash. Stir in pumpkin pie spice until well blended.

TROPICAL VEGGIE JUICE

makes 2 servings

⅛ pineapple, peeled

5 leaves kale

½ cucumber

½ cup coconut water

Juice pineapple, kale and cucumber. Stir in coconut water until well blended.

BACK TO YOUR ROOTS

EARTHLY DELIGHT

makes 3 servings

2 beets
2 carrots
2 parsnips
1 turnip
1 sweet potato

Juice beets, carrots, parsnips, turnip and sweet potato. Stir.

JICAMA FRUIT FROLIC

makes 2 servings

1½ cups strawberries, hulled

1 cup cut-up peeled jicama

1 apple

½ cucumber

2 sprigs fresh mint

Juice strawberries, jicama, apple, cucumber and mint. Stir.

KALE AND FRIENDS

makes 2 servings

3 carrots
2 stalks celery
1 apple
3 leaves kale
½ cup fresh parsley

Juice carrots, celery, apple, kale and parsley. Stir.

CLEVER CARROT COMBO

makes 1 serving

1 cup cut-up
   peeled jicama

½ pear

2 carrots

½ inch fresh ginger,
   peeled

Pinch ground
   red pepper
   (optional)

Juice jicama, pear, carrots and ginger. Stir in red pepper, if desired, until well blended.

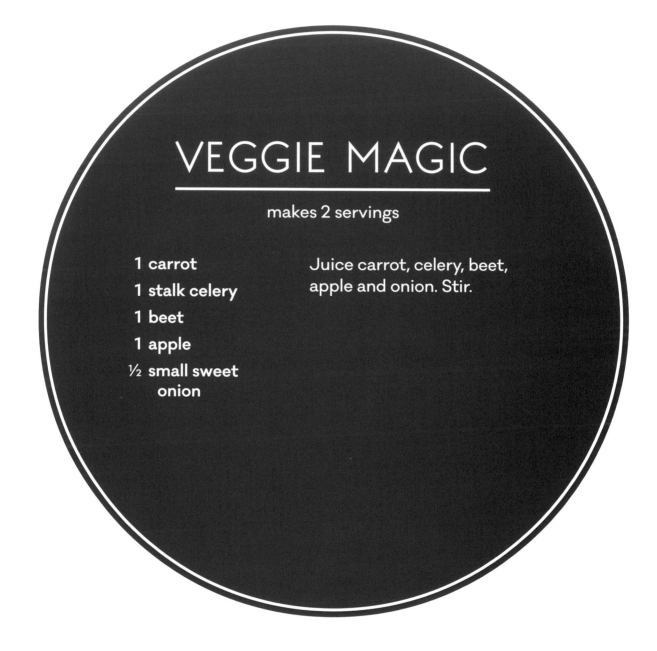

VEGGIE MAGIC

makes 2 servings

1 carrot
1 stalk celery
1 beet
1 apple
½ small sweet
onion

Juice carrot, celery, beet, apple and onion. Stir.

HANG LOOSE

makes 1 serving

5 carrots

2 radishes

½ inch fresh ginger,
   peeled

Juice carrots, radishes
and ginger. Stir.

PARSNIP PARTY

makes 2 servings

3 parsnips
1 apple
1 pear
½ bulb fennel
½ cup fresh parsley

Juice parsnips, apple, pear, fennel and parsley. Stir.

RUBY
APPLE STINGER

makes 2 servings

2 beets
2 carrots
½ apple
1 inch fresh ginger, peeled
¼ lemon, peeled

Juice beets, carrots, apple, ginger and lemon. Stir.

SWEET POTATO SPLASH

makes 4 servings

4 **apples**
1 **sweet potato**
1 **carrot**

Juice apples, sweet potato and carrot. Stir.

BIG GREEN WAVE

makes 2 servings

1 cucumber
1 green apple
2 stalks celery
½ bulb fennel
3 leaves kale

Juice cucumber, apple, celery, fennel and kale. Stir.

FIERY CUCUMBER BEET JUICE

makes 2 servings

1 cucumber

1 beet

1 lemon, peeled

1 inch fresh ginger, peeled

½ jalapeño pepper

Juice cucumber, beet, lemon, ginger and jalapeño pepper. Stir.

ROOT RECHARGE

makes 2 servings

2 parsnips
2 carrots
½ cucumber
1 lemon, peeled

Juice parsnips, carrots, cucumber and lemon. Stir.

PURPLE
PINEAPPLE JUICE

makes 2 servings

1 beet

1 pear

¼ pineapple,
  peeled

1 inch fresh ginger,
  peeled

Juice beet, pear, pineapple
and ginger. Stir.

BLENDER BREAKFASTS

BERRY TANGERINE DREAM

makes 3 servings

½ cup water

2 tangerines, peeled and seeded

2 cups frozen mixed berries

1 cup fresh pineapple chunks

2 teaspoons honey

Combine water, tangerines, mixed berries, pineapple and honey in blender; blend until smooth.

ORANGE APRICOT SUNSHINE

makes 2 servings

½ cup dried apricots

¾ cup water

1 navel orange, peeled and seeded

½ cup frozen mango chunks

½ teaspoon grated fresh ginger

Place apricots in small bowl; cover with hot water. Let stand 20 minutes; drain. Combine ¾ cup water, orange, mango, apricots and ginger in blender; blend until smooth.

GREEN CANTALOUPE QUENCHER

makes 2 servings

2 cups cantaloupe
  chunks

1 cup frozen
  pineapple
  chunks

1 cup baby
  spinach

1 tablespoon
  ground flaxseed

Combine cantaloupe, pineapple, spinach and flaxseed in blender; blend until smooth.

MANGO CITRUS SMOOTHIE

makes 2 servings

2 small tangerines

1 cup frozen mango chunks

¼ cup ice cubes

Juice of 1 lime

1 tablespoon honey

Grate peel from tangerines; peel tangerines. Combine tangerine sections and grated peel in blender with mango, ice, lime juice and honey; blend until smooth.

RISE 'N' SHINE

makes 2 servings

½ cup uncooked old-fashioned oats

1 cup orange juice

1 container (6 ounces) vanilla yogurt

½ cup vanilla soymilk

4 fresh strawberries, hulled

3 ice cubes

1 teaspoon ground cinnamon (optional)

Pour oats into blender; grind into fine crumbs. Add orange juice, yogurt, soymilk, strawberries, ice and cinnamon, if desired, to blender; blend until smooth.

CARROT CAKE SMOOTHIE

makes 1 serving

½ cup coconut water

3 medium carrots, peeled and cut into chunks (about 6 ounces)

½ banana

½ cup frozen pineapple chunks

1 teaspoon honey

⅛ teaspoon ground cinnamon

⅛ teaspoon ground ginger

Combine coconut water, carrots, banana, pineapple, honey, cinnamon and ginger in blender; blend until smooth.

ISLAND DELIGHT

makes 2 servings

1 cup unsweetened almond milk

1 frozen banana

½ cup frozen mango chunks

1 tablespoon almond butter

Combine almond milk, banana, mango and almond butter in blender; blend until smooth.

MORNING GLORY SMOOTHIE

makes 2 servings

1 pink or ruby
  red grapefruit,
  peeled, seeded
  and pith
  removed

¾ cup frozen
  strawberries

1 banana

1 teaspoon honey

Combine grapefruit, strawberries, banana and honey in blender; blend until smooth.

JUST PEACHY CANTALOUPE SMOOTHIE

makes 2 servings

¼ cup orange juice

2 cups frozen sliced peaches

1½ cups cantaloupe chunks

1 tablespoon almond butter

Combine orange juice, peaches, cantaloupe and almond butter in blender; blend until smooth.

RASPBERRY CHERRY BLEND

makes 2 servings

⅔ **cup apple juice**

1 **cup frozen raspberries**

1 **cup frozen dark sweet cherries, slightly thawed**

½ **avocado**

Combine apple juice, raspberries, cherries and avocado in blender; blend until smooth.

MANGO REVERIE

makes 2 servings

¾ cup unsweetened coconut milk

1 cup frozen mango chunks

½ orange, peeled and seeded

½ teaspoon vanilla

Combine coconut milk, mango, orange and vanilla in blender; blend until smooth.

BREAKFAST POM SMOOTHIE

makes 2 servings

¾ cup pomegranate juice

½ cup unsweetened almond milk

1 frozen banana

¼ cup sliced fresh strawberries

½ cup fresh blueberries

Combine pomegranate juice, almond milk, banana, strawberries and blueberries in blender; blend until smooth.

SUPERFOOD SMOOTHIES

REFRESH SMOOTHIE

makes 1 serving

½ cucumber, peeled, seeded and cut into chunks

1 cup frozen mixed berries

¼ cup ice cubes

1 tablespoon honey

Grated peel and juice of 1 lime

Combine cucumber, berries, ice, honey, lime peel and lime juice in blender; blend until smooth.

STRAWBANANA BLEND

makes 2 servings

½ **cup orange juice**

½ **banana**

½ **cup fresh strawberries, hulled**

¼ **avocado**

1½ **cups ice cubes**

Combine orange juice, banana, strawberries, avocado and ice in blender; blend until smooth.

BLUEBERRY APPLE BOOSTER

makes 2 servings

½ cup apple juice

1 Granny Smith apple, seeded and cut into chunks

1½ cups frozen blueberries

⅛ teaspoon ground allspice

Combine apple juice, apple, blueberries and allspice in blender; blend until smooth.

KIWI GREEN DREAM

makes 2 servings

¾ cup water

2 kiwis, peeled and quartered

½ cup frozen pineapple chunks

½ avocado

1 tablespoon chia seeds

Combine water, kiwis, pineapple and avocado in blender; blend until smooth. Add chia seeds; blend until smooth.

AUTUMN CELEBRATION

makes 2 servings

2 plums, pitted and cut into chunks

1 pear, seeded and cut into chunks

½ cup fresh or thawed frozen cranberries

¼ cup ice cubes

⅛ teaspoon ground ginger

⅛ teaspoon ground cinnamon

Combine plums, pear, cranberries, ice, ginger and cinnamon in blender; blend until smooth.

RASPBERRY RICHES

makes 2 servings

1 cup almond milk

2 cups frozen
 raspberries

½ avocado

2 tablespoons
 lemon juice

Combine almond milk, raspberries, avocado and lemon juice in blender; blend until smooth.

PURPLE PLEASER

makes 3 servings

½ cup water

2 cups seedless red grapes

2 cups frozen blackberries

2 cups baby spinach

½ cup ice cubes

¼ teaspoon ground cinnamon

Combine water, grapes, blackberries, spinach, ice and cinnamon in blender; blend until smooth.

BERRY CRANBERRY BLAST

makes 2 servings

1 cup water

1 cup frozen mixed berries

½ cup fresh or thawed frozen cranberries

½ avocado

1 tablespoon honey

½ teaspoon grated fresh ginger

Combine water, mixed berries, cranberries, avocado, honey and ginger in blender; blend until smooth.

GREEN ISLANDER SMOOTHIE

makes 2 servings

1 banana

1½ cups fresh pineapple chunks

1 cup loosely packed spinach

1 cup packed torn kale

2 cups ice cubes

Combine banana, pineapple, spinach, kale and ice in blender; blend until smooth.

SUPER BLUE SMOOTHIE

makes 2 servings

½ cup pomegranate juice

¼ cup water

¾ cup frozen blueberries

¾ cup frozen blackberries

½ avocado

2 teaspoons honey

Combine pomegranate juice, water, blueberries, blackberries, avocado and honey in blender; blend until smooth.

RUBY RED DELIGHT

makes 2 servings

¼ cup water

1 navel orange, peeled and seeded

1 medium beet, peeled and cut into chunks

½ cup seedless red grapes

½ cup frozen strawberries

¼ teaspoon ground ginger

Combine water, orange, beet, grapes, strawberries and ginger in blender; blend until smooth.

CHERRY ALMOND SMOOTHIE

makes 2 servings

½ cup almond milk

1½ cups frozen dark sweet cherries

½ banana

2 teaspoons almond butter

⅛ teaspoon ground cinnamon

Combine almond milk, cherries, banana, almond butter and cinnamon in blender; blend until smooth.

GREEN GOODNESS

SUPER SMOOTHIE

makes 1 serving

½ cup apple juice

1 cup packed torn kale

1 cup baby spinach

1 banana

1 cup ice cubes

Combine apple juice, kale, spinach, banana and ice in blender; blend until smooth.

GOING GREEN

makes 4 servings

¼ honeydew
  melon, rind
  removed and
  cut into chunks

4 kiwis, peeled
  and quartered

1 cup green
  seedless grapes

2 cups ice cubes

2 tablespoons
  honey

Combine honeydew, kiwis,
grapes, ice and honey in
blender; blend until smooth.

GREENS GALORE

makes 2 servings

¼ cup water

2 small Granny Smith apples, seeded and cut into chunks

1 cup baby spinach

⅓ seedless cucumber, peeled and cut into chunks (4-inch piece)

¼ cup ice cubes

⅓ cup fresh mint leaves (about 3 sprigs)

Combine water, apples, spinach, cucumber, ice and mint in blender; blend until smooth.

PEAR-AVOCADO SMOOTHIE

makes 2 servings

1 cup apple juice

1 pear, peeled, seeded and cut into chunks

½ avocado

1½ cups ice cubes

½ cup fresh mint leaves

2 tablespoons lime juice

Combine apple juice, pear, avocado, ice, mint and lime juice in blender; blend until smooth.

REFRESHING GREEN SMOOTHIE

makes 1 serving

¾ cup coconut milk

1 cup baby spinach

¾ cup frozen pineapple chunks

½ teaspoon grated lemon peel

Combine coconut milk, spinach, pineapple and lemon peel in blender; blend until smooth.

TANGY APPLE KALE SMOOTHIE

makes 3 servings

1 cup water

2 Granny Smith apples, seeded and cut into chunks

2 cups baby kale

1 frozen banana

Combine water, apples, kale and banana in blender; blend until smooth.

TRIPLE GREEN TREAT

makes 2 servings

2 cups seedless
   green grapes

1 kiwi, peeled
   and quartered

½ avocado

Combine grapes, kiwi and avocado in blender; blend until smooth.

GREEN PINEAPPLE PICK-ME-UP

makes 1 serving

½ cup frozen
 pineapple
 chunks

½ avocado

1 cup baby kale

1 tablespoon
 lime juice

1 teaspoon honey

Combine pineapple, avocado, kale, lime juice and honey in blender; blend until smooth.

SWEET SPINACH SENSATION

makes 2 servings

½ cup water

1 sweet red apple, seeded and cut into chunks

1 tangerine, peeled and seeded

1 cup frozen mango chunks

1 cup baby spinach

Combine water, apple, tangerine, mango and spinach in blender; blend until smooth.

GREEN DREAM

makes 1 serving

½ cup vanilla
   almond milk

¼ cup vanilla
   yogurt

1 cup loosely
   packed spinach

¼ avocado

1½ cups ice cubes

1 teaspoon lemon
   juice

1 teaspoon honey

Combine almond milk, yogurt,
spinach, avocado, ice, lemon
juice and honey in blender;
blend until smooth.

SWEET GREEN SUPREME

makes 2 servings

2 cups seedless green grapes

½ **frozen banana**

½ **cup baby kale**

½ **cup ice cubes**

Combine grapes, banana, kale and ice in blender; blend until smooth.

TROPICAL GREEN SMOOTHIE

makes 2 servings

½ cup orange juice

1 cup packed torn
   kale

1 cup frozen tropical
   fruit mix*

1 cup ice cubes

2 tablespoons honey
   or agave nectar

*Tropical fruit mix typically
contains pineapple, mango
and strawberries along with
other fruit.

Combine orange juice, kale,
fruit mix, ice and honey in
blender; blend until smooth.

METRIC CONVERSION CHART

VOLUME MEASUREMENTS (dry)

1/8 teaspoon = 0.5 mL
1/4 teaspoon = 1 mL
1/2 teaspoon = 2 mL
3/4 teaspoon = 4 mL
1 teaspoon = 5 mL
1 tablespoon = 15 mL
2 tablespoons = 30 mL
1/4 cup = 60 mL
1/3 cup = 75 mL
1/2 cup = 125 mL
2/3 cup = 150 mL
3/4 cup = 175 mL
1 cup = 250 mL
2 cups = 1 pint = 500 mL
3 cups = 750 mL
4 cups = 1 quart = 1 L

VOLUME MEASUREMENTS (fluid)

1 fluid ounce (2 tablespoons) = 30 mL
4 fluid ounces (1/2 cup) = 125 mL
8 fluid ounces (1 cup) = 250 mL
12 fluid ounces (1 1/2 cups) = 375 mL
16 fluid ounces (2 cups) = 500 mL

WEIGHTS (mass)

1/2 ounce = 15 g
1 ounce = 30 g
3 ounces = 90 g
4 ounces = 120 g
8 ounces = 225 g
10 ounces = 285 g
12 ounces = 360 g
16 ounces = 1 pound = 450 g

DIMENSIONS

1/16 inch = 2 mm
1/8 inch = 3 mm
1/4 inch = 6 mm
1/2 inch = 1.5 cm
3/4 inch = 2 cm
1 inch = 2.5 cm

OVEN TEMPERATURES

250°F = 120°C
275°F = 140°C
300°F = 150°C
325°F = 160°C
350°F = 180°C
375°F = 190°C
400°F = 200°C
425°F = 220°C
450°F = 230°C

BAKING PAN SIZES

Utensil	Size in Inches/Quarts	Metric Volume	Size in Centimeters
Baking or Cake Pan (square or rectangular)	8×8×2	2 L	20×20×5
	9×9×2	2.5 L	23×23×5
	12×8×2	3 L	30×20×5
	13×9×2	3.5 L	33×23×5
Loaf Pan	8×4×3	1.5 L	20×10×7
	9×5×3	2 L	23×13×7
Round Layer Cake Pan	8×1½	1.2 L	20×4
	9×1½	1.5 L	23×4
Pie Plate	8×1¼	750 mL	20×3
	9×1¼	1 L	23×3
Baking Dish or Casserole	1 quart	1 L	—
	1½ quart	1.5 L	—
	2 quart	2 L	—